HEAVENLY ®
HARVEST

SUPER-NATURALLY

The ABCs of Faith

PICTURE BOOK AND MEMORY GAME

GROWN

Scripture taken from the New King James Version®. Copyright © 1982
by Thomas Nelson. Used by permission. All rights reserved.

WestBow Press books may be ordered through booksellers or by contacting:

WestBow Press
A Division of Thomas Nelson & Zondervan
1663 Liberty Drive
Bloomington, IN 47403
www.westbowpress.com
1 (866) 928-1240

ISBN: 978-1-9736-3274-0 (sc)
ISBN: 978-1-9736-3275-7 (e)

Library of Congress Control Number: 2019904046

Print information available on the last page.

WestBow Press rev. date: 4/24/2019

THIS BOOK BELONGS TO:

_____

DESIGNED & ILLUSTRATED BY:

ATTENTIVELY
Armando Avocado
GROWN

Aa

Aa 01

247365

avocado

No.

1

one

"Let each of you look out not only for his own interests, but also for the interests of others."

Philippians 2:4

Bb 02
247365

Bb

blueberries

No.

2

two

"Now, Lord, look on their threats, and grant to Your servants that with all boldness they may speak Your word."

Acts 4:29

Cc

No.
3

three

carrots

"But whoever has this world's goods, and sees his brother in need, and shuts up his heart from him, how does the love of God abide in him?"

1John 3:17

DETERMINEDLY
Dario Dragonfruit
GROWN

Dd

HEAVENLY HARVEST
"The Freshest Supernatural Produce"

Dd 247365 ·04

No.

4

dragonfruit

four

"I have fought the good fight, I have finished the race, I have kept the faith."

2 Timothy 4:7

EXHORTINGLY

Emily Eggplant

GROWN

Ee

eggplant

No.

5

five

"Speak these things, exhort, and rebuke with all authority. Let no one despise you."

Titus 2:15

F f

fig

No.

6

.
SIX

"Now faith is the substance of things hoped for, the evidence of things not seen."

Hebrews 11:1

Gg

garlic

No.

7

seven

"I will both lie down in peace, and sleep; For You alone, O Lord, make me dwell in safety."

Psalms 4:8

HOSPITABLY
Holly Honeydew
GROWN

Hh

No.

8

honeydew

eight

"Do not forget to entertain strangers, for by so doing some have unwittingly entertained angels."

Hebrews 13:2

INDUSTRIOUSLY
Isobel Iceburg Lettuce
GROWN

I i 09

247365

Ii

iceburg lettuce

No.

9

nine

"He who gathers in summer is a wise son; He who sleeps in harvest is a son who causes shame."

Proverbs 10:5

J j

No.

10

Ten

jalapeño

"You will show me the path of life; In Your presence is fullness of joy; At Your right hand are pleasures forevermore."

Psalm 16:11

Kurtis Kiwi

Kk

kiwi

No.

11

eleven

"And be kind to one another, tenderhearted, forgiving one another, even as God in Christ forgave you."

Ephesians 4:32

LOVINGLY
Linus Lime
GROWN

Ll

No.

12

lime

twelve

"Greater love has no one than this, than to lay down one's life for his friends."

John 15:13

MEEKLY
Mirium Mushroom
GROWN

HEAVENLY HARVEST
"The Freshest Supernatural Produce"

Mm 13
247365

Mm

mushroom

No.

13

thirteen

"Let us not become conceited, provoking one another, envying one another."

Galations 5:26

NURTURINGLY
Nancy Nectarine
GROWN

Nn

Nn 14

247365

No.

14

nectarine

fourteen

"So he went to him and bandaged his wounds, pouring on oil and wine; and he set him on his own animal, brought him to an inn, and took care of him."

Luke 10:34

HEAVENLY HARVEST

"The Freshest Supernatural Produce"

Oo 15
247365

Oo

orange

No.

15

fifteen

"Children, obey your parents in the Lord, for this is right."
Ephesians 6:1

PATIENTLY
Penelope Pumpkin
GROWN

Pp 16

247365

Pp

No.

16

sixteen

pumpkin

"But let patience have its perfect work, that you may be perfect and complete, lacking nothing."

James 1:4

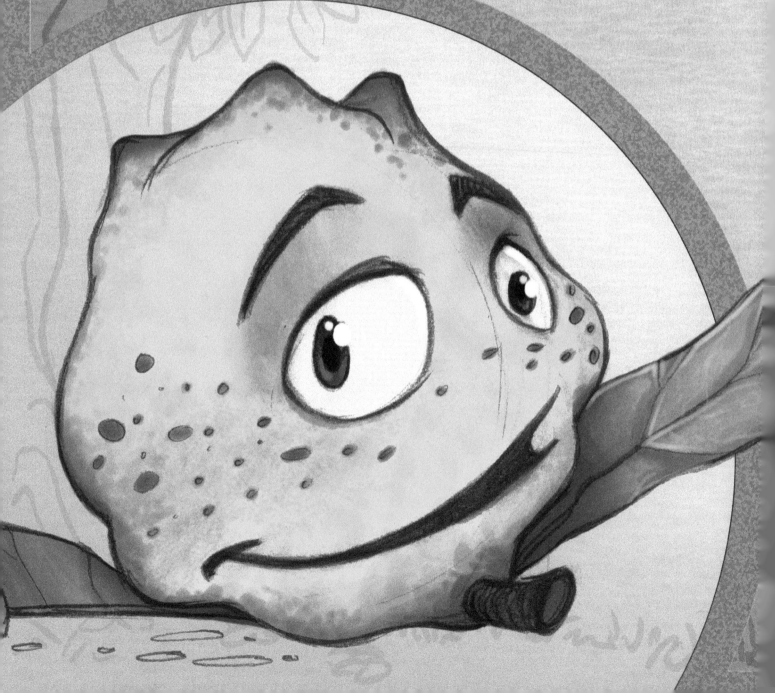

Qq 17

247365

Qq

No.

17

quince

seventeen

"Yet I had planted you a noble vine, a seed of highest quality."

Jeremiah 2:21a

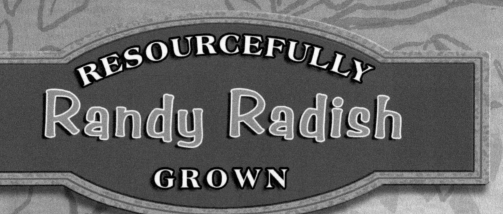

RESOURCEFULLY
Randy Radish
GROWN

R r

radish

No.

18

eighteen

"He who is faithful in what is least is faithful also in much; and he who is unjust in what is least is unjust also in much."

Luke 16:10

SELF-CONTROL
Samantha Strawberry
GROWN

S s

strawberries

No.

19

nineteen

"I say then: Walk in the Spirit, and you shall not fulfill the lust of the flesh."

Galatians 5:16

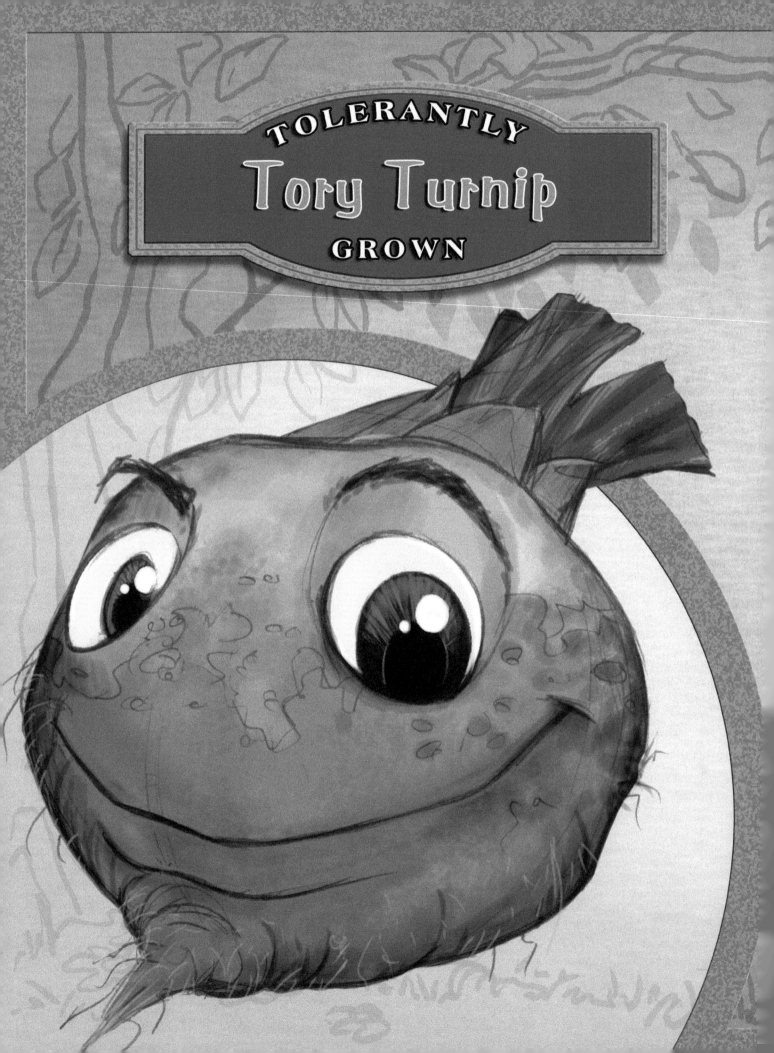

T t

HEAVENLY HARVEST
"The Freshest Supernatural Produce"

Tt 20
247365

No. 20

turnip

twenty

"Let nothing be done through selfish ambition or conceit, but in lowliness of mind let each esteem others better than himself."
Philippians 2:3

UNDERSTANDINGLY
Ursela Ugli
GROWN

Uu

No.

21

ugli

twenty-one

"For the Lord gives wisdom; From His mouth come knowledge and understanding;"

Proverbs 2:6

VIRTUOUSLY

Victoria Voavanga

GROWN

Vv

Vv 22

247365

No.

22

voavanga

twenty-two

"by which have been given to us exceedingly great and precious promises, that through these you may be partakers of the divine nature, having escaped the corruption that is in the world through lust."

2 Peter 1:4

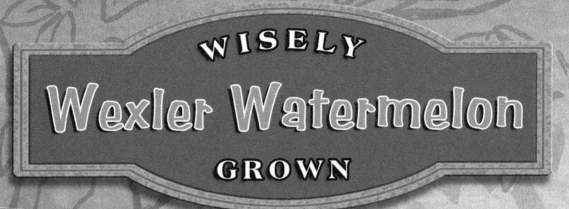

Ww

No.
23

watermelon

twenty-three

"The fear of the Lord is the beginning of wisdom, And the knowledge of the Holy One is understanding."

Proverbs 9:10

XENOPHILOUSLY
Xander Xigua
GROWN

Xx 24

247365

Xx

No. 24

xigua

twenty-four

" Let no one seek his own, but each one the other's well-being."

1 Corinthians 10:24

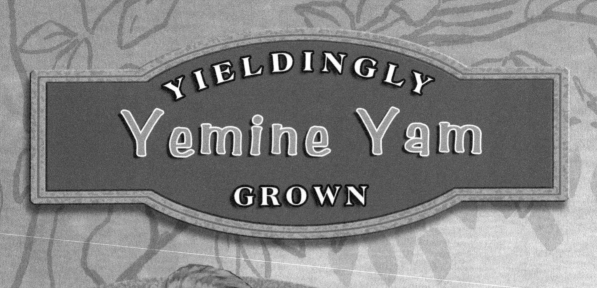

YIELDINGLY
Yemine Yam
GROWN

Yy

No.

25

yam

twenty-five

"... But these are the ones sown on good ground, those who hear the word, accept it, and bear fruit: some thirtyfold, some sixty, and some a hundred."

Mark 4:20

ZEALOUSLY

Zelda Zucchini

GROWN

Zz 26
247365

Z z

No.
26

zucchini

twenty-six

"And who is he who will harm you if you become followers of what is good?"

1 Peter 3:13

·Memory Game·

Psalms 77:11

16 | **P**

Penelope

P **p** | sixteen

pumpkin

INSTRUCTIONS:
1.) CUT OUT THE GAME PIECES ON THE NEXT SEVERAL PAGES.
2.) PLACE THEM ALL FACEDOWN ON A FLAT SURFACE AND MIX'EM UP.
3.) NOW TRY TO MATCH THE CARDS BY TURNING OVER ONLY TWO AT A TIME.
4.) WHEN YOU HAVE FOUND A PAIR, PLACE THEM ASIDE AND CONTINUE.
5.) PLAY BY YOURSELF, OR TAKE TURNS WITH OTHER PLAYERS.
6.) THE ONE WITH THE MOST FOUND PAIRS WINS!

1 A a

Armando | avocado

2 B b

Billy & Bobby | blueberries

3 C c

Christopher | carrots

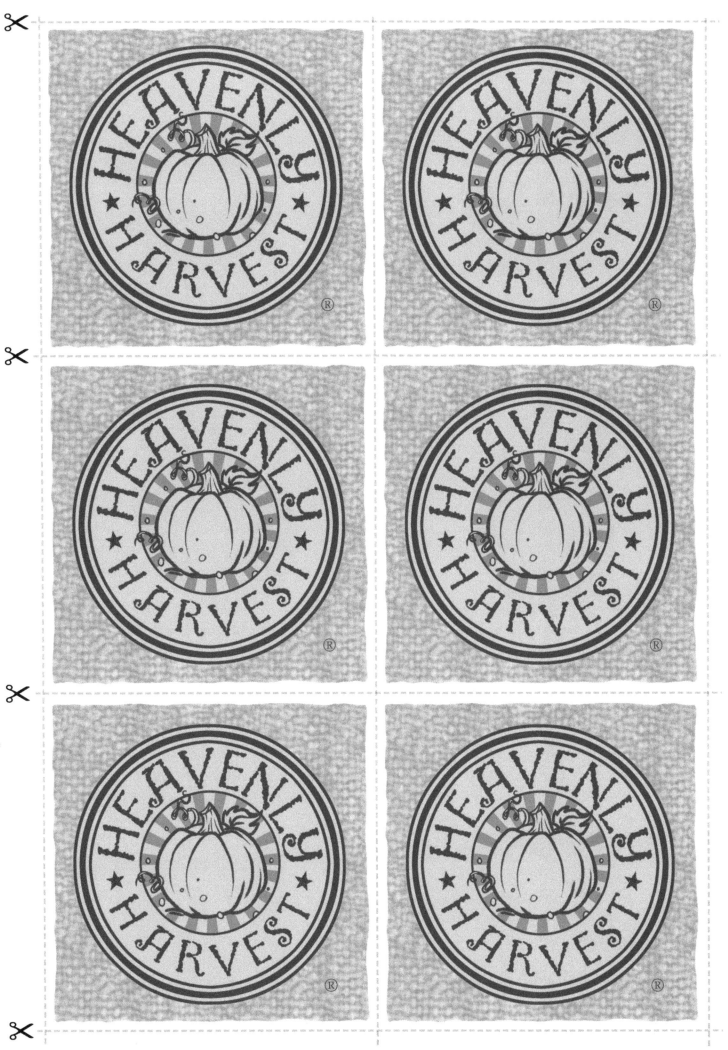

4 D d

Dario

dragonfruit

5 E e

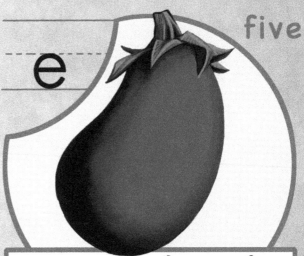

Emily

eggplant

6 F f

Finkle

fig

With a pair of scissors or utility knife, safely cut out each of the cards

7

G g

Gabriel

garlic

H h

Holly

honeydew

I i

nine

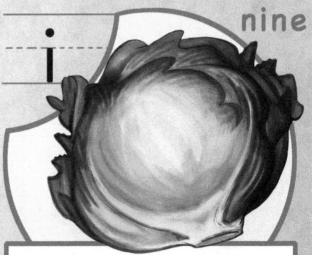

Isobel

iceberg lettuce

eight

With a pair of scissors or utility knife, safely cut out each of the cards.

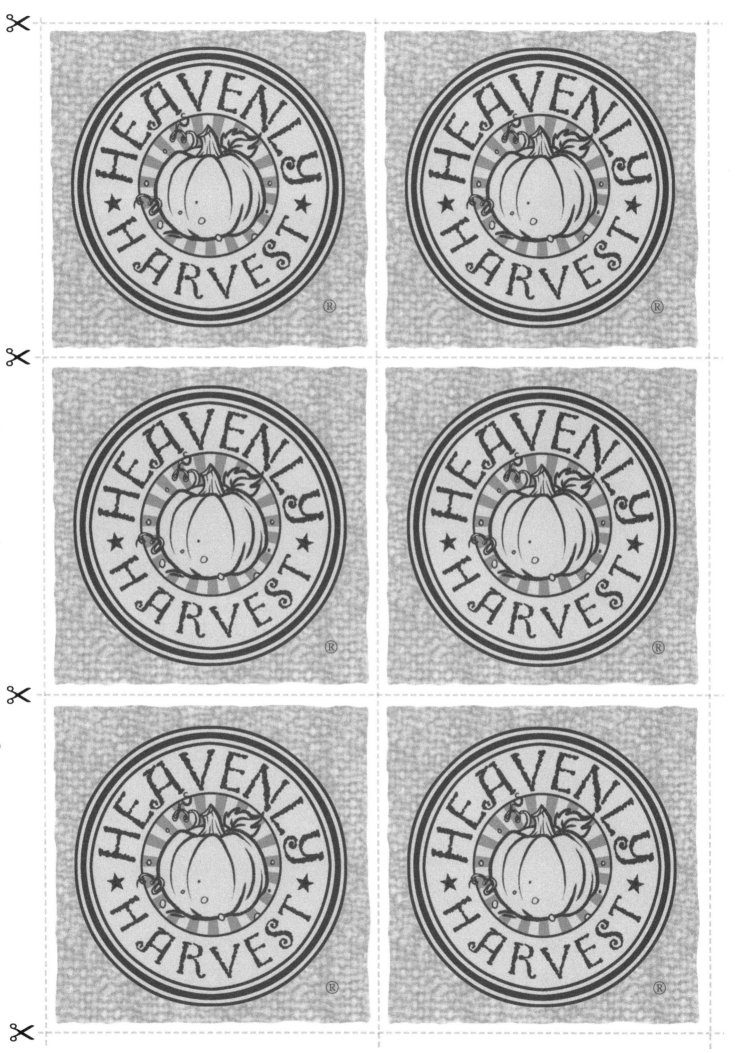

10 J j

Jamie

jalapeño

11 K k

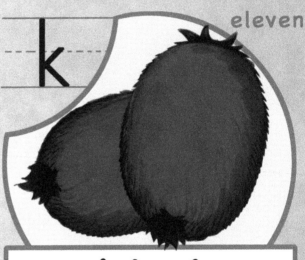

Kurtis

kiwi

12 L l

Linus

lime

With a pair of scissors or utility knife, safely cut out each of the cards.

M m

Miriam

mushroom

N n

Nancy

nectarine

O o

Odile

orange

With a pair of scissors or utility knife, safely cut out each of the cards.

16

P

Penelope

sixteen

p

pumpkin

17

Q

Quentin

seventeen

q

quince

18

R

Randy

eighteen

r

radish

With a pair of scissors or utility knife, safely cut out each of the cards.

19

S s

Samantha **strawberries**

20

T t

 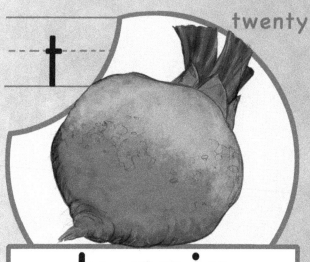

Tory **turnip**

21

U u

 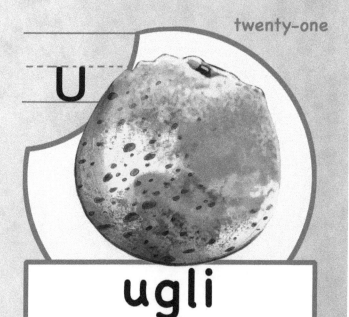

Ursela **ugli**

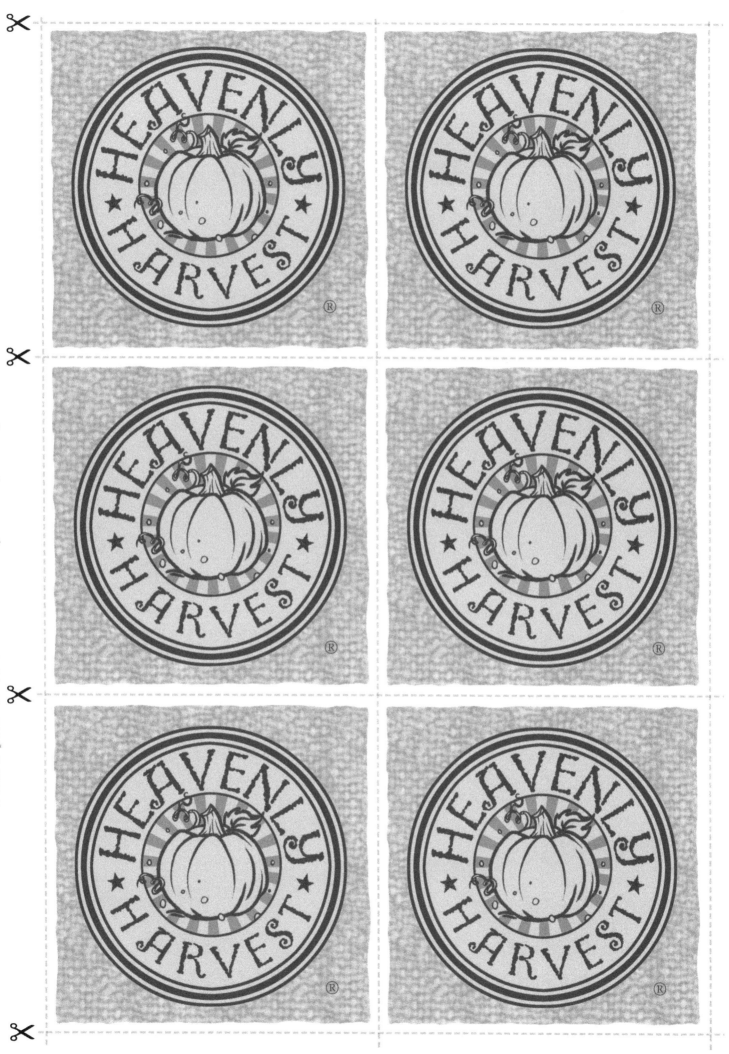

With a pair of scissors or utility knife, safely cut out each of the cards.

22 V v

Victoria

voavanga

23 W w

Wexler

watermelon

24 X x

Xander

xigua

25

Y

Yemine

y

yam

26

Z

Zelda

z

zucchini

draw
you

first initial

last initial

favorite
food

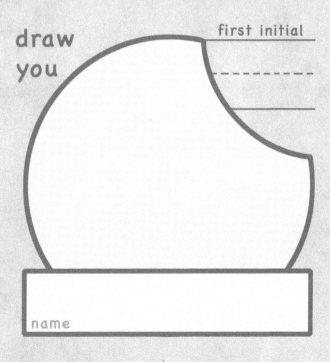

name

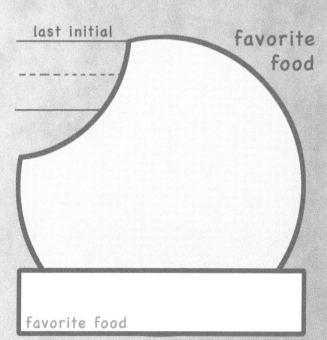

favorite food

THIS COLOR KEY IS TO HELP YOU INDENTIFY WHICH CHARACTER BELONGS TO WHICH FAMILY OF FOODS. 'THESE FOODS ARE ALL GOOD FOR YOU TO EAT!

HEAVENLY
· Fruits & Berries ·
HARVEST

HEAVENLY
· Vegetables ·
HARVEST

HEAVENLY
· Fungus ·
HARVEST

HEAVENLY
· Root Vegetables ·
HARVEST

*WHILE THESE FRUITS AND VEGETABLES ARE A PART OF A HEALTHY DIET, IT IS IMPORTANT NOT TO EAT BERRIES, MUSHROOMS, OR PLANTS FOUND IN THE WILD UNLESS AN ADULT SAYS IT'S OK. MANY PLANTS CAN BE POISONOUS, AND MAKE YOU VERY SICK!

PATIENTLY
Penelope Pumpkin
GROWN

Nutrition Facts
Penelope Pumpkin   (patience)   16

Penelope Pumpkin is a patient part
of the "Fruits of the Spirit", and of a
well balanced spiritual diet.

Penelope is a good friend and teacher.

She always makes time to give to those
who need her.

Penelope never yells or loses her
temper with those around her.

She sits and listens before she acts.

Penelope never rushes to judgement.

The pumpkin is a member of the squash family. They
have a thick yellow or orange skin and deep ridges from
the stem to the bottom. They are mostly grown in North
America, and have a bright yellow or orange trumpet-like
bloom. They are often associated with the autumn season
and the harvest. A pumpkin is the mascot for the Heavenly
Harvest logo for that very reason.

The letter "P" is the 16th letter of the alphabet.

OF THE SPIRIT · HEAVENLY HARVEST

Pp

PATIENTLY
Penelope Pumpkin
GROWN

No.
16

Product of
HEAVEN

HEAVENLY HARVEST

Who Are We?

Proverbs 22:6

Penelope patiently waited
for the little mouse
to tell his story.

James 1:2-6

Heavenly Harvest® is designed to be a faith-based learning franchise that incorporates life tools from scripture with language, arts, health, and wellness. By design, it links the "fruits" of the Spirit with healthy physical and spiritual growth through recognition, consumption, and practice. Because of the engaging characters and story lines, children will enjoy reading and writing, all the while being introduced to the importance of reading labels on packaged food items, and learning about what they eat. Each character in Heavenly Harvest® represents a Godly character trait with a corresponding verse from the Bible, a letter, and a number.

H.H. Parents have multiple online learning tools available to them. Supplemental web based content in this book is accessible from any tablet or mobile device equipped with a QR code reader. Parents are able to access printable coloring sheets, and activity worksheets online to augment what students get in their public school or homeschool classroom.

Visit Heavenly Harvest® online to find additional content, printable activities, recipes, and products for your classroom or home.

If you have encountered any problems with this book or its links to online content, please contact Heavenly Harvest® via the "Contact" link on the website.

www.heavenlyharvesting.com

HEAVENLY HARVEST

·How It Works·

Job 37:7

| POINT CAMERA AT THE QR CODE. | SCAN THE QR CODE. | THE QR CODE WILL LOAD AUTOMATICALLY. | THE EXCLUSIVE WEB PAGE WILL LOAD IN MOMENTS. |

SPECIAL NOTE:
CODES USED IN THIS BOOK ARE LINKED TO
EXCLUSIVE ONLINE CONTENT THAT CAN
BE ACCESSED ONLY THROUGH THIS BOOK!

CPSIA information can be obtained
at www.ICGtesting.com
Printed in the USA
BVHW021200010519
547059BV00009B/109/P